P🐾W PRINTS
ON THE COUCH

PAW PRINTS ON THE COUCH

KIM LENGLING

Lead Author: Kim Lengling
Book Cover Design: Kim Lengling
Stock photo(s)-Canva
Publisher: Kim Lengling Author
Printed in the United States of America
First Print Edition, 2023

ISBN: 9798392911684

TABLE OF CONTENTS

FOREWORD

When Kim announced she had written a new book, of course, I felt compelled to endorse her!

As fellow Podcast Hosts, we met and had an amazing connection and conversation about dogs!

I am a Certified Life Coach, Speaker, Podcast Host, and Author of two award-winning books on dogs. So, I can honestly share that Kim joins me in our love and understanding of how our canine friends give examples of living our best lives and loving life unconditionally.

She has compassion, passion, and an all-out love for life despite her own struggles as a veteran living with PTSD. She strives to share hope through everything she does, from public speaking to being a TV show host, radio show host, and podcast host to help others.

After publishing several books in the anthology format, her writing experience is a beautiful addition to another anthology of stories, including the struggles, heartbreaks, and inspiration that we all experience as humans and the unconditional love and joy that pets bring to enhance and help our lives.

Maureen Scanlon

Award-Winning Author of two books: **My Dog is More Enlightened Than I Am** and **My Dog is my Relationship Coach**. Available on Amazon.

INTRODUCTION

Kim Lengling

I don't know about you, but my life would be too quiet without a dog.

I know it is the same feeling many people have with all sorts of pets; dogs, cats, snakes, horses, goats, whatever animal you may have, bringing you love and joy.

How amazing that we are blessed to care for and love these animals.

The stories within this book are those of pet parents. They share a small glimpse of life with their pets. They share the joy their pets bring, and yes, they share the sadness of loss when they have to say goodbye.

Having a pet in our lives is a privilege that brings great rewards. However, since animals can't speak for themselves, we each take on a responsibility as pet parents to advocate for them and provide the love, support, and resources they need to live healthy, happy lives.

Being a pet parent is a big responsibility, and it is one that I take on gladly. My goodness, how their sweet souls have enriched my life and those of the pet parents in this book. If you are a pet parent, I am sure your life has also been enriched!

Enjoy the read and give your pet an extra hug today.

EXTRA INTRA-DUCTION

Dexter

HI. I'm Dexter!

But sometimes my Lady Mum calls me, "Leave it be," "Drop it," or "Monkey Butt."

She's got lots of names for me. She's kinda funny that way.

Ya know another way humans are funny? They don't like smelling stuff on the ground, and they don't even wanna try to eat deer poop or fox poop or any kinda poop.

They don't like rolling in the grass or stuff they might find in a field. My Lady Mum says, "Dexter! No, you're gonna be a mess and stink!"

I tell her it smells neat, and it's fun to roll around on the ground, but she still won't do it.

So, my Lady Mum, that's what I call her, she's a good human. She got me from the place with too much smell and noise. It was kinda scary there cuz I didn't know why I was there. The humans kept calling me "a stray." I'm not sure what that means.

I was kinda scared when I first met my Lady Mum. Humans seem so big, and sometimes they aren't very nice. But she seemed nice. I sniffed at her and figured out she was a good person. She smelled like home. I really wanted a home, but fer some reason, I was in this loud place with hard floors.

I've been with my Lady Mum fer a while now and I have all kinds of jobs. One of them is "Office Manager."

That's where my Lady Mum sits in a chair in front of the small TV thing and pushes all those little buttons real fast. When I'm workin, I watch her, take a nap, or look out the window and tell her what I see. I also tell her when she needs to go outside fer a walk. Humans need their walks, and it is a portant job to be sure they know when it's time to go outside.

Whoops! Lady Mum says to quit babbling cuz I'm sposed to be intra-ducing what yer gonna read.

M'kay, so, this thing you got in your hands? It's called a book, and it's got all kinds of stories of humans and their pets. There are dogs and cats and even a horse! I've never met a horse, but Lady Mum says some live down the road, and maybe we can meet 'em sometime.

Ya wanna know something else? I learned I'm not the only one who was picked to live with a human. Lots of others were picked by their humans to come live with them. Some from a loud place like I was at, and some just cuz they showed up, and the humans let 'em stay. How neat is that?

I don't know what else to say, and I'm not sure what a intra-duc-tion is, so I'm just gonna be done now. I'm ready to take my Lady Mum fer a walk anyway.

I hope ya like the stories and that you love your pet as much as my Lady Mum loves me! I love her too cuz she gives me treats.

It's nice having a human.

Dexter

"The love and loyalty of a pet is a bond that can never be broken."

Unknown

DIGGER

THE UNFORGETTABLE ONE

Kim Lengling

For those who love dogs and have had one or more, you'll understand when I say, "There is always that one. The one you will think of regularly for the rest of your days."

I've had several dogs throughout my life and have loved them all equally. But for some reason, one will forever enter my mind and remain a part of my life and heart.

For me, that was Digger. He came into my life as a rescue at 13 weeks old. The shelter informed us he had been "adopted" twice but returned.

I never understood that. How could someone return a puppy? But, over time, I realized Digger's journey was just as it should be so he would end up with me.

From the start, he was smart and took to training like a duck to water. We trained him using German commands, and his ability to catch nuance and tone was amazing. When teaching him something new, he got it the first time around.

Digger was with me for 14 years, and how blessed my daughter and I were to have him! He brought so much joy and energy into our lives.

Eventually, my daughter grew up and went on to begin her own life. After that, Digger became my constant companion. Running errands? He came with me. Going to the Park? He would get excited, grab his leash in his mouth, thunder down the deck stairs, and race to the garage door to prance in circles until I caught up.

I would regularly attend public events with Digger as my sidekick. As time passed, everyone who knew Digger would greet him affectionately. Now, whether he wanted anything to do with people at times was apparent. Depending on his mood, he would tolerate some or be excited and playful with others. He had his moods and his unique personality. With a regal tilt of his head, you would know whether he wanted your attention. At times, it was comical and had me laughing out loud over the years.

He became known as the Mighty Black Dog and The Keeper of The Watch. He earned the Mighty Black Dog moniker as he came up to mid-thigh on me and weighed in at 105 pounds. When standing on his hind legs to give me a "hug," he stood over 5 feet tall, and we were eye to eye.

He was a protector, hence the nicknames, The Mighty Black Dog and Keeper of the Watch.

I always followed his lead when meeting people. If Digger liked a person, he was relaxed. If he felt something off about someone, he would tense up and stand by my side or stand directly in front of me, showing his teeth. He would not growl; he would puff up and show his teeth. That little trick of his stopped several unseemly people from approaching over the years!

We had a routine of a minimum of two half-hour to 45-minute walks per day. As a large dog, Digger needed his exercise and time outside; honestly, I needed those walks just as much as Digger did. Over the years, we walked hundreds of miles together. Goodness, the miles we put on our paws and feet!

We would walk through the fields and woods surrounding our area, otherwise known as "the Realm." We also took trips to area parks and lakes. If there was a body of water, no matter the size, Digger was in it. He was a great swimmer but preferred to stay close to shore and swim in large circles. When it was time to head home, he would not want to leave the water. He would stand just far enough away from me in the water and stare, silently conveying that he was not ready to leave.

Without fail, I would laugh and say, "Digger, are you trying to convince me to stay with the power of your stare?" But darned if that stare didn't work. He would get to keep swimming for a while longer.

It was no different with puddles, whether they were big or small. Digger would either stand in them or sit right down in them and employ the power of his stare. His stare was something else!

Digger had so much compassion and empathy. It was uncanny how in tune he was. If he thought I was sad or having a bad day, he instinctively knew when to nudge me or "tell" me we needed to go for a walk.

I live with PTSD (Post Traumatic Stress), and Digger knew when and how to settle me down. Goodness, the hugs my big guy endured and the tears that fell upon his fur over the years! His patience and care were something I never took for granted. I knew what a blessing it was to have him in my life.

He would hop up on the couch in the evenings to lay beside me. At other times he would think he was still small and sit his 105 pounds on my lap.

Digger's personality was huge, and everyone who met him fell in love with him.

I began sharing Digger Stories online—stories of The Mighty Black Dog and The Keeper of The Watch.

They were conversations between him and me, with Digger always sharing some wisdom.

His stories were about our adventures, as he liked to call them. Stories of our trips to the park or the lake. Stories of chasing critters from the yard and protecting his Mum. Stories of his numerous run-ins with skunks. He never learned to leave them alone! That was one thing I would remind him of, "Digger, you are the smartest dog on the planet, yet you continue to chase and catch skunks; why?"

In return, I would get a turn of the head or a snort as he walked away from me, leaving a trail of stink in his wake.

Those who read the stories would regularly ask what Digger would share next. It was as if the people who read the conversations forgot that a human was writing them!

I would share the comments with Digger, earning me a snort and a look as if to say, "Mum, of course, people know how smart I am."

I could tell what he was thinking by looking at his face. He had quite a sense of humor and no small bit of sarcasm. It was his eyes. Those eyes shared so much expression, almost human.

It is difficult to convey what an awesome dog Digger was in 1500 words or less, but I hope you can get a feel for him and his personality.

His story will continue. All those conversations and stories I mentioned earlier. I've kept those stories and plan to put them in a separate book so Digger's wit and wisdom can bless others! I think he would get a kick out of it. At the very least, he would consider it something that should have been done sooner.

Goodness, I loved that dog and will miss him for the rest of my days. But as life happens and we move forward, a spot in our heart opens, and you may feel the nudge that another dog out there needs your love and care.

Six sad and lonely months after I said goodbye to Digger, I received that nudge and adopted a skinny, ill, and skittish two-year-old from the same shelter Digger came from. I named him Dexter, and his story continues to unfold.

"My goal in life is to be half as good as my dog thinks I am."

Unknown

DEXTER

A YOUNG'EN ENTERS THE REALM

Kim Lengling

Six months after I said a heart-wrenching goodbye to my Digger, I felt a nudge in my heart. A nudge that said, "There's a dog out there that needs you."

Driving to work, I felt those words, "There's a dog out there that needs you." My first reaction was, "No. I can't do it again. It's too hard."

The nudge came again, and I replied, "I can't. It hurts too much!"

Once at work, those words wouldn't leave my mind. So, I went online to see what dogs may be available at my local shelter. There was only one dog, which was unusual.

There was a picture of this dog with the following information: Male, Shepard Mix, approximately three years old, stray, no background.

What caught my attention was his coloring. He had a black head, a fawn-colored body, white feet, a white patch on his chest, and one brown eye and one ice-blue eye.

He was so unique looking. I decided to call the shelter and set a time to meet him. I had resigned myself to the fact that I would probably be getting a dog, but the dog would have to choose me. It had to be the right fit. I did not tell anyone I was even thinking of getting a dog. I needed this process to be between the dog and me.

The next evening, I went to the shelter to meet this young boy. I was escorted into the "meet and greet" room and asked to wait. A volunteer eventually brought this boy into the room. He was thin and quite skittish. He didn't want to leave the volunteer's side and kept his nose to the door as if he wanted to leave.

I sat down on the floor to be at his level. I didn't say anything or move a muscle. I wanted him to feel comfortable enough to approach me on his own.

After a few minutes, the volunteer left this scared boy with me, and the waiting began. Me sitting on a cold cement floor as this dog sniffed the air, paced back and forth, pawed at the door, and eventually sat down with his head hanging.

After a few minutes, his curiosity overcame him, and he tentatively approached me. First, he would sniff near my hand and back away. Then, he would walk to my other side, sniff near my hand, and back away.

I continued to be silent and still.

After about 10 minutes, this young boy approached me again. He sniffed near my hand, went to my other side, and sniffed my shoulder. Finally, he tentatively sat beside me and, within a few seconds, leaned his entire body against mine and placed his head upon my shoulder, looking up at me with that one ice-blue eye.

I softly whispered, "Ah, so there you are. You're coming home with me, aren't you?"

He chose me. Now it was a matter of getting the fees, shots, and paperwork. I had to wait 48 hours before I could pick him up and bring him home.

Returning home that night, I second-guessed myself. Was I ready for another dog? Could I give the love this scared and sickly dog would need while still missing my Digger so much? There was no information on his background. How would I know if he would be a good dog for me?

The questions whirled around my mind causing me to have a sleepless night.

The following evening after work, I stopped at the store to get food, a new leash, collar, dog bed, and a toy. But I wanted to see his personality before I went too overboard!

The night I picked him up, the volunteer brought him out. He seemed excited to see me, as if he knew he was finally going "home."

As we left the shelter and approached my vehicle, without hesitation, he jumped in the back seat of my car, sat down, and faced forward as if to say, "Okay. I'm ready!"

That first night was filled with small whines from Dexter with me whispering throughout the night to reassure him that he was okay. He was home.

I had come up with the name Dexter and would use it while talking to him as he explored the house, using his new name regularly. Unfortunately, no one knew his original name since he was found as a stray.

The first two weeks were a time of getting used to each other, and Dexter was beginning to feel better. He had been quite ill when I adopted him. So, it was a tenuous time, along with a new home, a new person, and still feeling fearful.

It took Dexter three months to fully settle in, and his personality began to shine through. And what a character he is!

I had been used to caring for a senior dog for the past several years, and it took some getting used to a younger, more energetic one. But we soon got into a routine and learned each other's ways.

Training began immediately, and Dexter took to it quite well. I trained him using German commands along with hand commands. Right away, I noticed certain hand gestures caused him to duck and cringe. I realized he might have been abused, and I quickly changed my hand gestures to ones that would not seem threatening and gently assured him there was no need to fear me.

It was all so different with Dexter. I was used to Digger and his personality. I had to remind myself that Dexter was not my previous dog and had his own personality and quirks.

Another thing I noticed after a few days; Dexter never made noise. He didn't bark, growl, howl, or anything.

When I adopted him, I noticed his neck was swollen and often wondered if he had been tied out or mistreated in some way using a collar.

Finally, with his cringing at hand commands and his swollen neck, I realized this sweet soul had been treated poorly.

I decided not to use a collar with him but instead a harness. The swelling in his neck went down after a few weeks, and he slowly began to "talk."

Now, four years later, Dexter is a VERY vocal boy and lets me know, in no uncertain terms, when it is time to get up for the day, time to go outside, time to eat, and time for a treat. He is strong-willed, filled with energy and attitude, and is quite a character.

He loves everyone. He is a horrible protection dog and can't catch a ball if his life depended on it. He'll jump into the UPS or FedX truck without hesitation and chase any animal that is smaller than him.

He terrorizes the birds at the bird feeders, has been sprayed by skunks five times since he has been with me, hogs the couch, and continues to eat deer poop out in the woods, and I love him just as he is.

He is a wonderful addition to a house that became too quiet after a sad goodbye to my Digger, the Mighty Black Dog.

So often, with the loss of a pet, we tell ourselves we can't do it again. It hurts too much.

I have had the same thought, but then I am reminded of all the animals out there who desperately need a loving home, and my mind and heart experience a shift.

Dogs can and do bring so much joy, compassion, and love. Their hearts are pure. Knowing their lives are short hurts, but I've realized something. An animal comes into our lives for a reason. They have a job to do, which is love. They do their job well. So very well.

Keep your heart open and give a hurting soul a love-filled home, and you will be blessed beyond measure.

"*Animals are such agreeable friends. They ask no questions, they pass no criticisms.*"

George Eliot

MIDNIGHT

GETTING BACK ON THE HORSE

Anita Buzzy-Prentiss

We were cantering in the arena. The horse tripped and fell hard and fast to his knees. I've often ridden through trips as an experienced equestrian, but this one was different. It happened so quickly.

I was flung into the air and landed on my shoulder and head. I immediately knew something was broken. I was afraid to move. Slowly, I came to a kneeling position and felt a bone sticking out weirdly. My collarbone was broken.

My horse scrambled up, shook the dirt off, and ran away, stirrups flying. He was fine. I was in shock, and the pain was mind-numbing.

I was rushed to the hospital in an ambulance, and it was determined my clavicle was broken in multiple places. I needed surgery. A metal plate with five screws was inserted to hold my clavicle together. Luckily my helmet prevented me from incurring a head injury.

After months of grueling physical therapy, I knew I had to get back on the horse.

As I climbed on, I was shaking like a leaf. I immediately knew I needed to get off once I was up there. I needed a break. I had to leave one of the things I truly loved to do.

I was done for now. I had been pushing, trying, and pretending everything was okay. But I had lost the joy of riding a horse that wasn't a good match for me. I had known this for a while before the accident. I fell out of touch with my reason for riding horses and needed separation and space for understanding.

I couldn't think clearly. Every cell in my body told me to step away, so I had to listen. The memory of my fall and how weak, confused, and anxious I felt when I tried to ride again made my decision. My inner voice was saying, step away for a while.

It was a sad time in my life. I had gotten away from the initial reason I loved being around horses. I was caught up in riding in horse shows, winning ribbons, switching to different horses and barns, training with different trainers, competing, and searching for something I wasn't finding. What was it?

I missed my loving connection with my first horse many years ago. Her name was Midnight, and I loved spending time with her. When I wasn't with her, I would daydream about her.

I wanted to cry as I sifted through memories of the simple things and how far I'd come from my initial joy of being around horses. Would I ever feel that kind of love again?

This grief and confusion in my emotions came into my body deeply and turned into chronic migraines, blocked business growth, and depression. I felt like I was painted into a corner and didn't know how to get out. It felt like I had lost my joy and didn't know how to get it back. I was afraid to go riding because I was afraid I would get hurt or that I would, once again, get swept up in my competing mentality.

What now? What else makes me happy?

Watching performers at Cirque du Soleil on the silks gave me goosebumps. The combination of daring feats, bravery, freedom, strength, power, and control balanced with gracefulness—like riding a horse! Could I do that? But I was scared to death of being upside down or even having both feet off the ground!

Facing this fear with curiosity and playfulness, I knew I needed to get out of my head and into my body in a creative way that didn't involve horses (yet). So, I started going to an "antigravity" class on silk hammocks.

My fear of heights and being upside down led to initial misery! The first time I was hanging upside down, I became nauseous and dizzy and, at times, had to spend time in the bathroom slapping my face with cold water to help myself feel better. I felt exhausted for the rest of the day, but something kept bringing me back. There was a tingle of excitement and fun after every class—a little dose of danger—but the feeling that I could conquer my fear and get stronger every time made me smile. The biggest thing that brought me back was that I felt safe there.

Each class got a little bit easier! Baby steps. The teacher and the people in the class were supportive and clapped for every tiny improvement I made—a celebration of each small win. Of course, I couldn't do some parts of the class, but I would watch and think I might do that someday! The dizziness and nausea went away eventually, and my intuition was telling me: Maybe this is just what I needed to get stronger and more compassionate with my self-confidence, not pushing, but instead with gentleness, patience, and in small steps.

Instead of running from my discomfort, I stuck with it. What is this trying to teach me? When I thought about horses, I still felt scared. I wasn't ready to try again. Would it ever be possible to get back on a horse? I imagined it in my mind one day, and instead of feeling dread in the pit of my stomach, I started to get those butterflies of excitement again. I knew I could do it when I was ready!

Trusting my body's cues that I wanted to return to this anti-gravity class helped me understand that I was doing the right thing—working through my fear and growing stronger. I felt like I was slowly getting back in touch with myself in a deep yet gentle way.

During the pandemic, the studio shut down, which meant no more classes. I decided to get my own silks. I became comfortable with the silks and had fun with them! I hung around with my daughters laughing and playing together, or just laid in the hammock listening to relaxing music. I felt comfy and safe there. When I finally returned to the class, I could do everything I was so afraid to do before! I felt confident. I left the studio and felt like skipping down the street, feeling like a super badass!

Because I overcame my fears and turned them into something familiar and safe, I could start thinking about horses again. Could I return and be sincere to my boundaries? Could I find the right horse to ride, take it slow, speak up for myself, and make sensible choices so I wouldn't get hurt again? Maybe I could make a horse friend, enjoy my time with them, and not end up pushing, striving, and becoming all weird again.

The day I started thinking of this possibility, I saw a post from a barn that needed "experienced riders for their lesson horses," I felt like my name should have been printed there in capital letters. I realized that if I focused on my fear and ignored my joy for another day (and never rode again), I would be heartbroken for the rest of my life.

There is a fine line between "Do you want to try again?" and "Do you want to be done?" Are you just frustrated, or is this just not right for you? It's okay either way. There's no right or wrong choice. We need to trust what feels right at that moment.

Loving horses and spending time with them was something born in me. Horses have been the catalyst for deep lessons throughout my entire life. I need quality time with them to be at my best.

You must be strong yet calm and truly present in their presence; otherwise, you can get hurt. It can be overwhelming or scary, and not everyone can do this.

Being around horses is a humbling experience. You must be patient, dedicated, subtle, and speak clearly and effectively, most of the time with body language. Yet, to connect with these majestic beings (or to your highest self), you must be clear-minded and celebrate small successes.

Getting stuck in the ego, rushing, or using too much force will interfere with enjoying the process because we attach too much to the outcome of whatever we're doing.

Taking time away from horses and finding my way back helped me realize that I need my sacred time with these beautiful animals to be in tune with the best part of myself.

"Dogs feel very strongly that they should always go with you in the car, in case the need should arise for them to bark violently at nothing, right in your ear."

Dave Barry

DIAMOND

"Until one has loved an animal, a part of one's soul remains unawakened."
Antaole France

DIAMOND WAS A GIRL'S BEST FRIEND

Michelle Jones

My soul animal inspired me to write about our time together. Diamond was the best friend anyone could have. Over 14.5 years ago, my furry friend entered my life. Ultimately, the puppy that was stolen to save her life became my biggest lifesaver. The fact that she was so small and had a huge head made me a little nervous, and I don't have much experience with dogs, so that made me apprehensive. Learning how to balance a college education and an adult job was challenging. Responsibility and patience were lessons I learned from Diamond. I have always had a passion for animals. The experience of being a pet parent started at a young age for me.

When I was six, my mother let me get a cat as a birthday present. I've been a pet cat parent ever since; Sarah, my long-haired calico cat, lived a short life because she was sickly from the start. When Sarah passed away, my dad took me to the Humane Society, where we rescued an orange tabby. Because she chased her tail when I brought her home, I named her Spinner.

Spinner was my favorite. Her ten years of friendship were filled with me putting clothes on her, pushing her in a carriage, and caring for her. Spinner sadly passed away in my senior year of high school, and my heart was broken. A year passed without having a pet. My boyfriend at the time adopted a cat for me when I was in college and kept it at his house while I lived in student housing. That cat is still with me today, and her name is Dolce. While she isn't the friendliest cat, I love her very much.

Even though I became so attached to Diamond, it's almost impossible to believe I was against keeping her initially. In my childhood, I feared dogs because I assumed they would bite me. The boyfriend I had in college worked in a pet store. One day, he called me to come to pick him up early from work. He ran out quickly as I pulled up to the store where he worked. The jacket he was wearing was bulging. He told me that I should drive my car as quickly as possible. I was confused about what was going on, and I asked him what the rush was about. There was only one thing he kept saying, "Drive!". Driving out of the parking lot, I saw a small black head peeking out of his jacket. It was an adorable puppy that was a mix of a pit bull and a black lab. I asked him what was going on! He explained to me that when people return pets, they are deemed unadoptable and euthanized. That was the last day of his employment at this company. My boyfriend had pretty much stolen a dog, so I was freaking out and asked him what we would do. "We're keeping her," he said. Black Diamond is the name he gave her.

Because I grew up with cats, I had never experienced dogs. I didn't know what to expect. In all honesty, I was petrified. Puppies love to play, and often teeth are involved in playing. It was frightening to hold her. I thought she would bite me. Considering the stereotype that dogs chase cats, I was also concerned she would hurt my cat. I have a feeling my cat may have been a dog in a past life. When Dolce met Diamond, she acted like a professional boxer. As if doing a 1-2 jab, Dolce got up on her hind legs and swatted at Diamond's face. Diamond would run to us in hopes that we could provide her with protection. As long as she lived, this would be their dynamic. Although Diamond and Dolce would occasionally snuggle in bed together when nobody was looking.

As a result of spending time with Diamond, we developed a strong bond. When I had class, she went to doggy daycare and had a great time. She loved it at daycare, especially when I dropped her off, and she pranced into the building without noticing me or looking back. During that time, I was unaware that Diamond was teaching me the value of patience and responsibility.

Through every major event in my life, Diamond was with me, including my dad's stroke, graduation, marriage, relocation, divorce, heartbreaks, and more. I am grateful to Diamond for enriching my adult life.

Even though I tried my best to be a responsible pet parent, I wasn't always successful.

One of my most memorable camping trips will always be my first. It was Diamond and I's first camping trip together. My partner and I decided to canoe on the lake on this sunny, warm day. It was a beautiful day. We also brought a bottle of wine, as we wanted to enjoy the day. It is important to realize that the mere fact that something appears romantic on screen does not signify that it will be romantic in reality. The wine spilled after a short time. Diamond began licking the liquid from the bottom of the boat as if it were water. In the beginning, we did not notice anything as we rowed along, enjoying the ride. However, as soon as we got out of the canoe, we realized she appeared unbalanced. She wasn't quite getting into the truck at first, so I thought it might be due to her sea legs, but as she continued to struggle, I realized there might be something else going on. She didn't have sea legs, but instead, she was drunk. I felt awful.

Having Diamond as my unofficial emotional support dog was a great privilege. It was as if she had a sense of my emotions. She knew when I was scared, upset, or worried.

I welcomed another dog into my small family a year into my marriage. Hugo, a yorkie-min pincher mix, expanded our family. There was a special bond between Hugo and his big sister Diamond. Since he loved her so much, he sometimes annoyed her. His favorite activity was playing, often resulting in him biting Diamond's hind legs. When Diamond became tired of Hugo, she would slowly sit on him. Resting on him for a few minutes was like a break for her. As Diamond led the way, Hugo followed suit, always one step behind her, and loved to be in the same room as her.

Despite Diamond's 65 pounds and fierce appearance, she feared everything, including plastic bags, blue tarps, and Santa Claus. But, despite that, they conquered the world together. Diamond, Dolce, and Hugo were my three fur babies; they were like family members to me. It was a blessing to be their mother.

Diamond and I enjoyed sunbathing together. Diamond taught me the value of unconditional love. Having her around made me feel safe and loved. I would wake up to find her lying next to me the nights I went to sleep feeling sad. She would give me kisses and cuddle up to me. She kept showing me love when I couldn't show myself love. It was my privilege to have her as a best friend. Diamond was a friend who loved me when I forgot to love myself.

Diamond and I shared 14.5 years together. Although she isn't physically here with me, she is tattooed on my leg, which makes me feel like she is a part of my day-to-day life. She has even visited me in my dreams on occasion. Despite loving her all her life, I will miss her for the rest of my life. I believe all dogs go to heaven. I will miss her until I see her again. It was Diamond who was this girl's best friend.

"Cats have it all—admiration, an endless sleep, and company only when they want it."

Rod McKuen

RIZZO

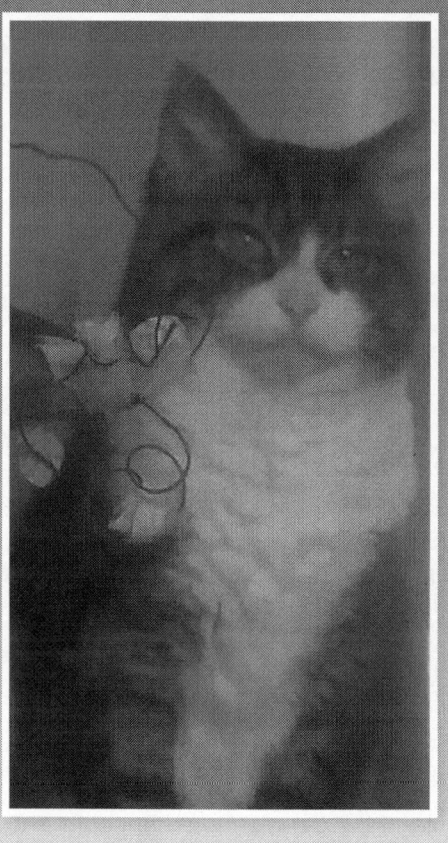

"The smallest feline is a masterpiece"
Leonardo da Vinci

WHERE PATHS COLLIDE

- -

Andrea Kebort

Some moments in Life are destined to become notable long before we know they are. This was true of that late fall day in November of 2005.

Our oldest was settled in as a college freshman, and we were experiencing our first taste of learning what it felt like to let go; to let a baby bird fly away. We were looking forward to her Thanksgiving break, as having everyone home would feel normal again.

We were soaking in the day and caught a quick glimpse of this curious cross-eyed kitty peeking through the glass panes of our kitchen door. Such a spirit surrounded this new friend and made this moment feel like it was destined to be a pivotal part of our history.

My memory recorded Valentine's Day as the day we would have a closer encounter with this tabby feline. Prior to this day, the sporadic glimpses continued, and we were never close enough to tell this visitor's gender. We had, however, thought the stripes seemed to be growing wider.

Our new friend was a very pregnant female, and where she came from was a mystery.

She would come and go, and we learned that she was a friend to several of our neighbors. She would saunter up to doors and ask to be invited inside. She sat for a while, checked in on her human friends, and then asked to leave again. This routine continued until late February.

Our furry pal was sticking around our yard and had adopted our storage barn as her home, and we realized she needed a name. Rizzo seemed like a spectacular name for her—after a character from 'Grease.'

We already had two cats in our house, and Rizzo seemed to be content and safe tucked away in our barn, so it was there she stayed and where she gave birth to five beautiful kittens in the wee hours of March 8, 2006.

Two males and three female kittens graced our lives that spring. We watched Abby, Gunther, Polly, Elphaba, and Chet as they devoted themselves to entertaining us. Our family had front-row lawn seats to this most spectacular live show, and we beheld them for hours as they pranced, frolicked, and wrestled.

It was no secret that our relationship with our family next door was rocky—non-existent, even. However, this slowly changed after we invited them to meet the babies. The bad times faded into the background as we all shared in watching as the kittens whiled the summer days away. It was as though Rizzo had been sent here to help us reconnect. This was an extraordinary blessing because my sister-in-law had passed away from a brain tumor a few years later. This reconnection, combined with my sister-in-law's sickness, is why my youngest daughter attended medical school. She is now an ER doctor saving many lives—never again to feel helpless in an emergency.

Rizzo's intelligence level was a cut above the rest. Over time we would see numerous examples of her intelligence and sixth sense as we sharpened this human-to-cat connection.

One afternoon, I was overwhelmed by the feeling that I needed to go check on the kittens. I found that little Polly was in distress; she had been walking across boards in the rafters and slipped and fell in between two boards. She was hanging by her neck and squirming madly in mid-air as she tried desperately to free herself. I had no clue how long she had been hanging there, but Rizzo ran to me and nipped gently at the back of my legs with undeniable intent as if to implore me to help her baby. I climbed up and got Polly down without incident, and thankfully she was fine.

Rizzo was most grateful, and our relationship blossomed as the trust level exploded. We adopted her and her daughter Abby and gave them loving homes—friends adopted the other four kittens.

Winter came, and since Rizzo and Abby were both so very friendly, we moved them into our garage, where they would be warm from the cold and safe from the dangerous country environment.

They were both heavily bonded to us, and every morning when my husband needed to move his truck out of the garage to go to work, we would catch them and hold them so he could safely back up his truck without running the risk of backing over one of them. Abby even got in the truck with my husband sometimes while he backed up. She would excitedly hop from window to window while he moved—until he would carry her back into the garage again. Naturally, the kitties looked forward to this time and sometimes playfully ran and hid from us to spice up the routine.

Rizzo was incredibly street-smart and had an uncanny ability to sense earthly matters before they happened. In August of 2011, we were concerned because she had been hiding underneath our garage's shelving units and would not come out—not even to eat. Later in the day, the news reported an earthquake in Pennsylvania; about an hour later, Rizzo ventured out of hiding and returned to acting her old self. I have to believe she sensed the seismic activity.

The garage was like a giant kitty playhouse with windows for the cats. They seemed to enjoy their routines and lives as they would climb all over the shelves and rafters. They had beds for warmth and were out of the wind, but one winter was particularly cold for an extended spell, so we took a risk and brought them inside the house with our other two resident cats. Everyone was vaccinated and healthy, so it seemed safe to give it a try.

One of our resident cats was a territorial alpha cat, so we had to ease into this transition. Rizzo and Abby stayed in our daughter's bedroom while she was at college. Gradually, they all became accustomed to one another, and new hierarchies were established over time. Even when the fur would fly, they unquestionably helped to fill our empty nest.

Sweet Rizzo loved everyone but was particularly bonded to my husband. We noticed that she'd always wanted to be with him when he was home. She wanted to lie on him and only him. She was getting old, so we did our best to give her what she wanted.

In the fall of 2019, after my husband's yearly physical, we learned that he had prostate cancer—he had probably had it for several years. After what we had witnessed with Rizzo hiding before the earthquake hit our area, I couldn't help but think she sensed something about him—perhaps his smell or vibe felt different to her. I believe she was trying to heal him.

My husband's full body scan in February revealed the cancer was isolated to his prostate. The morning of his scan, Rizzo refused food and was not her usual happy self she had been her entire seventeen or eighteen years.

My husband's surgery was scheduled, and Rizzo went to the veterinarian. Unfortunately, we learned she was suffering from pancreatitis and kidney issues. She was given an anti-nausea injection, and we bought special food to help support her kidney function.

We gave the meds a few days to work, but she was still refusing to eat anything. We had found her on her side, unable to get up, clearly in distress. It's never good when cats, masters at disguising weakness, show their discomfort.

In the days that followed, we returned to the veterinarian as soon as we could get an appointment. Typically, administering anti-nausea medicine is successful, but it did not help her at all. To look at her, she did not appear to be in pain all the time, but I could tell she was scared, and we knew she would have pain in the future if we allowed these health issues to progress.

We never knew her exact age but suspected she was around two or three years old when she came to us that one momentous spring. She had given us many memories, endless love, and undeniable support. She was our furry guardian who wanted to be sure my husband, her best friend, would be safe before her time was through.

With the situation that was at our feet, letting go became the only decent option—she deserved rest and peace. She closed her eyes that cold, sad late February day and was gone.

Rizzo's path led her to us, where she helped us find our path, and we are forever grateful to her.

Well done, my furry friend, well done.

"In ancient times, cats were worshipped as gods; they have not forgotten this."

Terry Pratchett

PAPI

*"The cat has complete emotional honesty—
an attribute not often found in humans."*
Ernest Hemingway

JUST ONE OF THE BOYS

Andrea Kebort

Sometimes growing tomatoes turns into much more than you'd ever expect.

Spring finally had arrived, but along with it came the endless list of chores. With winter now a mere memory, it seemed as though everything was alive again. I had dreamed of my garden and what I would plant in it all winter.

With my tomato plants in the ground, my husband had headed to the old storage barn to find as many tomato cages as he could. Yet, he returned and stood in front of me in the garden, empty-handed, with a look of boy-like wonder on his face.

"So, no tomato cages?" I quipped with a shrug. I followed him through the yard in anticipation of an explanation for the awe written on his face.

I entered the barn and began to pan the scene in and around the storage area, and it was there that I saw six glowing green eyeballs staring back at me for the first time. "Oh, no, not again!" I exclaimed.

Those eyes belonged to three curious but very fearful, mother-less-for-the-moment kittens. This was not our first rodeo when it came to stray kitten wrangling, but it was not expected this time—then again, it never is.

As they cowered, we saw all three were black and white with various markings on their faces and little bodies. We did not dare touch them as we did not want the mother cat to move them—this we had learned from experience, and even with the mess in this little outbuilding, we knew they were relatively safe there from predators.

The sun-filled sapphire morning skies made it easy for me to creep around like paparazzi as I desperately willed my shutter to capture glimpses of their innocence and pure unadulterated antics. On the other hand, I was all but certain my fluttering heart would be so loud it would reveal all my glorious human awkwardness as I slinked around behind trees.

After snapping about a million photos, I learned that six eyes were an underestimation; there were eight little eyes as there were four kittens, not three. We also learned that though momma kitty was practically a kitten herself, she was such an exemplary mother to her little feline apprentices day in and day out.

I am a firm believer in giving all animals names, so Mom became Stella, and her mini-me became Junior. The one with a dark smudge mark became—what else?—Smudge; another became Ziggy, and I called the big-eared fourth kitten Gizmo.

We watched them grow for most of the summer and became aware that they were leaving the confines of the storage barn and venturing out with mom and sometimes on their own. There were worrisome stints in which we would not see any of them for a few days, but they would always come back with new ways to entertain us—including and not limited to evening firefly hunting.

The last time we saw Stella and the four kittens together at one time was at the end of July, as mom was leading them out into what I imagined was a Kitty Survival 101 Training Camp. They all fell in step with their drill sergeant, who was only slightly larger than they were.

The end of summer was approaching quickly, and changes were afoot in early to mid-August. I did not learn until weeks later that Stella and three of the kittens had been trapped by neighbors and taken to an animal shelter; Stella had been spayed and released after a brief healing period.

The three kittens at the shelter and Momma were all vaccinated and neutered, as all three trapped kittens were male. They all tested negative for FeLV and FIV and were slowly coming around to becoming socialized; we had never really gotten the chance because their mom was so feral.

Unfortunately, kitten number four, the one I'd been calling Ziggy because of his markings, was left behind, as the neighbors who trapped the rest did not know that he existed. His socialization seemed promising, but the animal shelter that had his brothers was not interested in him—very sad, I know.

I had a home lined up for him if I could successfully socialize him, so we worked hard to find small ways to ingratiate ourselves with this little orphaned furball. We had smashing success at getting him to not only like but love humans, so we moved him into the garage and crated him at night while we awaited his neutering appointment.

Unfortunately, the promise of a new home fell through, but because he had proved himself to be an amazingly friendly and very vocal little fella, my husband and I decided we would keep him. We thought he and our ten-year-old female cat Dutch would be a good match and good company for each other.

We changed his name to Little Papi as the zigzagged markings on his head grew to look more like a number seven. Our favorite Boston Red Sox baseball player, David Ortiz, wore the number thirty-four, which adds up to seven, so it was a done deal; we had our very own lovable Little Papi.

With each passing day, we fell more in love with this little guy as he is one of the only males I have ever known who seemed to be able to out-talk me and enjoy doing so.

His neutering appointment and all vaccinations and blood tests were booked. I had just lost two of my senior cats in the months before Little Papi's surgery, and the pain of losing them was so bad I had told myself I didn't want any more pets. So, hearing words I dreaded, "Little Papi has tested positive for feline leukemia," floored me; it took my breath away.

My hearing, commonsense and ability to breathe were stripped away at that moment; this was too much, and it felt like I was right back to the daily cycle of never-ending uncertainty—the ugly limbo where I had been for two years with my two old girls: Annie, who died from breast cancer, and Abby, who had chronic vomiting and constipation issues. I watched them both slowly slip away.

I tried to absorb the words being spoken, but all I could hear was my inner voice screaming, "Oh, no, oh, no!"—over and over again.

I had some decisions to make and was so angry because it didn't seem fair at all that this little kitty with a lucky number seven on his head was the only one who tested positive. He was around four months old when he was on his own, old enough to mate, and I had learned that this is among the leading methods of transmission.

My heart was broken, and though I had read a lot about FeLV, its transmission, and the vaccines that exist to help prevent its spread, I felt I had to put Ms. Dutch first. Unfortunately, the vaccine is not a guarantee; it felt like we were all in the middle of a no-win situation at this point.

An extremely kind and knowledgeable man told me his desire to adopt Papi if he tested positive again using a DNA test. Much to my dismay, the day before Thanksgiving, I learned that he was progressively positive, but he was, in fact, lucky to have this opportunity to live in a home with other positive and negative cats, where he would be given a chance to thrive.

I beg this human race to do the right and responsible thing and spay and neuter animals in their care! I beg humans to have empathy and compassion for the plight of homeless animals. Most communities offer discounted spay/neuter and vaccine clinics.

Animals roaming outside will mate as this is their instinct, but it should also be the instinct of mankind to want to protect God's creation from harm and disease. With FeLV and FIV transmission largely occurring while breeding, there would be much less transmission if cats were spayed and neutered.

A FeLV diagnosis is not an automatic death sentence and shouldn't be treated as such. Many resources offer guidance and information about feline leukemia, and humans need to understand the importance of prevention. Please remember that many cats that test positive can live long and happy lives like any other cat.

I wanted Papi's paw prints on my home's couch, floors, and windows, but this was not meant to be. Nevertheless, I hope our story will forever be on the conscience of humanity.

Little Papi is definitely not a tomato, but he is a Better Boy (tomato variety) for allowing us to help cultivate his destiny.

"No matter how little money and how few possessions you own, having a pet makes you rich."

Louis Sabin

LEO

LEO

Kristi Mallory

It was 9 pm on a fall evening in South Texas. I was sitting on my sofa, eagerly awaiting the arrival of Leo, the two-year-old black and white Boston Terrier. He was rescued from a kill shelter in Oklahoma and was being chauffeured to his forever home with my kids and me.

Traffic slowed the drive for my friend who was transporting Leo, and they arrived much later than expected. My kids had gone to bed and would have an exciting meet and greet with Leo the following day, but I was awake and eagerly awaiting his arrival.

Suddenly, the door opened, and Leo burst through. Before I could stand, he jumped on the sofa and ran from one armrest to the next. RIGHT ACROSS MY LAP!

He claimed me before I even had the chance to greet him. And so began his habit of jumping onto places he was not invited.

If the barstools were not pushed into the kitchen island just right, Leo had the athletic ability to jump on them to get to the countertop and devour whatever was there.

He would also jump into the fourth chair at the dinner table to join us for meals. He would look at us as if saying, "Where's my dinner plate?".

My kids taught Leo to jump from the chair to the kitchen tabletop. The way the sun flooded through the window onto the kitchen table made it the perfect sunbathing spot.

I often walked into the kitchen to find him clambering to jump off the table. He would then glance at me, like a guilty child, and pretend that nothing ever happened.

He patrolled the backyard like a veteran police officer with years on the force looking for 4-legged animals like possums and squirrels. Our favorite family joke was: What is black, white, and green and has eight legs? The answer is Leo with a lizard in his mouth.

Of course, if we needed his skills to protect us from a 2-legged intruder, we knew we would be out of luck. But, on the other hand, he was always friendly to people.

This funny dog loved chocolate and built up quite a tolerance for it against my wishes and best efforts to keep him safe. We learned quickly never to leave chocolate around, even at the bottom of a bag, in the upstairs closet where Leo was not allowed.

He lived through three significant indulgences, including a solid chocolate Santa, half a bag of kisses (foil and all), and a bag of M&M's that he found while rummaging through a guest's luggage. That third episode finally taught him a lesson and curbed his cravings.

After that, he mostly stuck with the savory people-food he could find. This mainly happened when we left our meals unattended at the kitchen table or didn't quite get the chairs pushed under the kitchen counter.

The kitchen is the heart of our house and was Leo's domain. If food was dropped on the floor, it was best to leave it. Leo would pounce on it so quickly that there was no chance of recovering it.

Leo was a leaner. If you sat beside him on the couch, he would lean into you and enjoy your presence. He never demanded attention and would sometimes gently paw at you. That was his way of telling you to pet him.

He was so afraid of thunderstorms that we wondered if he escaped some close calls living through tornadoes while a resident of Oklahoma. We imagined him seeking shelter under a tree, looking up and watching the swirling storms pass over his head. He was always allowed to sleep in my bed on stormy nights, as if I had a choice.

He was not a fan of fireworks, so we ensured he was well protected around the 4th of July. While we enjoyed the fireworks show outside, he had a designated spot in the house where he could lean into whichever family member volunteered to be inside.

He rarely barked, so on the occasion we heard him, we listened. He had a muted, guttural growl that he used when identifying uninvited guests in the yard. It might have sounded scary to others, but we knew the truth.

Leo was stingy with his kisses. If you used the command "Kiss Kiss," he would barely stick his tongue out to give you the tiniest, skimpiest kiss.

We learned within the first few weeks of having Leo; never to open the front door without having him on a leash or restrained. He would push his way through if there was the slightest opening of a door or gate and sprint as if his life depended on it.

Despite our efforts, we could never curb this behavior. He was a Houdini at finding his way out and would run for his life whenever he got the chance.

It only took us a few times to figure out that if we chased after him on foot, the faster he would run. So, we developed a system.

When we discovered he was out of the yard, the kids would head out on foot after him. I would immediately jump in the car and drive the neighborhood slowly, with the windows down, hollering his name.

Once spotted, all we had to do was open the car door, call his name, and he would come running and jump in. This was our magic trick to outsmart that little Houdini, and it worked like a charm. The funny thing is, we had the opportunity to meet a handful of strangers in Leo's lifetime who figured out the same thing.

One summer evening, the kids and I were playing a board game, and the phone rang. I didn't recognize the number, but I am so glad I decided to answer.

The lady on the other end asked me if I had a dog named Leo. Gasp! That rascal had managed to get out of the backyard and run two miles away! This kind stranger was walking into a restaurant for dinner and saw Leo running across the parking lot.

Leo willingly jumped into her car to wait for our arrival. I gratefully bought her a round of drinks for her kindness.

Leo was the second dog I had in my lifetime. I waited 25 years after the death of my first before I got another.

When I was a teenager, our beloved dog got sick and died while my parents were out of town. It was traumatic. Her death left a mark on my heart; it took me years to recover before I was ready for another pet.

That's why I was surprised at the end of Leo's life when his health took a sharp turn. I knew exactly what I needed to do.

My kids and I hoped for better news from the doctor about Leo, but the plan was to keep him out of pain. And when there were no more options left and hard choices had to be made, it was the easiest decision to make and the hardest thing to do to let him go.

I have memories of my son climbing into the kennel at the veterinary hospital to snuggle with Leo one last time. The image of my daughter bravely saying her final goodbyes is burned into my mind.

Leo taught us that part of loving is saying goodbye. He generously gave so much to us and imprinted his funny personality in our hearts forever.

"Animals are such agreeable
friends—they ask no questions,
they pass no criticisms."

George Eliot

ROXIE

ROXIE

Cierra Meenachan

I woke up this morning and started my usual routine: I prep myself for the day, feed my cat, and let the dog out before work. Watching Roxie move, stretch and wobble onto her feet stirred some feelings of sadness within me. Roxie is currently a 16-year-old Pomeranian Yorkie and my best friend. I adopted her when she was about ten weeks old.

She was a tiny little thing. She weighed about three pounds, and the thought of owning a dog was far from my mind. Initially, she was a birthday gift for my mother because she wanted a Yorkie. It turns out that Roxie chose me, and since then, we have had so many adventures. These adventures are what taught me many things about myself.

I learned patience when learning to house train. Roxie was hard to house-train. I didn't do much research about Pomeranians or Yorkies before my decision. I started crate training her after weeks of researching ways to house-train puppies. This required so much patience and a steady schedule. Thankfully, I had help from my family, but she was my responsibility. She eventually improved with training but always needed the crate overnight.

This was not only because she was stubborn. It was because small dogs have tiny bladders.

I learned sometimes it's not about what you can do but what you will do to make things happen for yourself. I remember there was a time I wasn't home often. When I turned eighteen, I just wanted to hang out with my friends, and Roxie was usually left behind for my family to take care of her. I decided that I didn't have the time to give. She deserved more attention and more time with someone who could meet her needs. My best friend's mom, Michelle, said she would take her, and I knew she would be loved and cared for. So, I dropped her off and went to work. I was so sad when I got home, and she wasn't there to greet me at the door. I called Michelle crying, telling her that I missed my dog. She laughed and kindly said, "She is your dog; she's been looking for you. Come and get her if you want her." I rushed out of the house and picked her up. From that point, Roxie and I went everywhere together. Since she was so tiny, I would squeeze her into my coat, and she would ride inside it with me. When we were in the car, she would sleep in the hood of my coat until we reached our destination. I made sure to spend time with her and play with her so we could be together forever.

I learned to be more responsible and compassionate. People say that dogs and their owners share similar features and characteristics. I am a big people person and want to talk all day. I do not like being alone and enjoy having a companion with me. I went to work one day and came home to find out Roxie had gone missing. My siblings left her outside to hang out on the porch with Evey; she loved to sunbathe. Roxie, however, got bored and took off searching for a new friend. I was so worried; I searched the neighborhood and cried, thinking of what could have happened to her. Finally, someone told me to contact the police department, and luckily a neighbor spotted her wandering and took her into their home to ensure she was safe. I vowed I would never lose her again when I got her back! I was so grateful that someone found her and was honest about it.

I learned to be fierce and to protect what I love. Our first move together was with my friend Amber and her daughter Alyssa. During our stay there, Roxie would relax on the porch with me. She was almost always a good listener until a man and his German Shepard were walking down the street one day. I didn't see them, but Roxie did, and she took off attempting to chase him. In a huge panic, I ran down the steps yelling and telling her to come back. Luckily, the large dog was very obedient. The owner told him to sit, and he didn't budge. From that point forward, I was more diligent about her training. It took some time before the training took. We had one more incident where she tried to hitch a ride with the garbage truck. If you have seen the back of a garbage truck, there is a space where the men who grab the cans stand, and she hopped right in when he jumped off. I ran down and called her over. She hopped off and came back. The man had a good laugh for the day as he patted her head and took off to the next destination down the road.

I learned to read all the information on the packaging and labels. We moved into our first place with a big backyard, and Roxie loved it. I didn't realize that the previous occupants had a horrible flea infestation. I used Frontline at the time, and it worked great. I didn't know that the medicine only worked for adult fleas. I let her previous month's medicine lapse by only three days! I had no idea what to do for her. That was the year I learned Roxie was allergic to fleas. She lost her fur, and I had to nurse her back to health. Finally, I found a new flea medication that got rid of any bug that could cause her harm.

I have learned so much about love and appreciation as a pet owner. We moved into an apartment, and I loved that my living room window happened to be a sliding door. It allowed Roxie to look out the window and enjoy the view. This view usually consisted of neighbors coming in and out of the building, so they got to know her face. Once, I came home from my 10-hour shift, and my neighbor said, "You know, she is always in that window. She waits for you to come home every day." That statement occasionally comes back and reminds me of how much she loves me. She would wait in the window for me to return home everywhere we moved. I make sure I play with her as much as possible and greet her daily. Even now, as a little old lady, she has the heart of a young pup who looks to run and play to her heart's content.

Having a pet has changed my life significantly. I do not have children, so Roxie is my child. She has been here for every move, every relationship, and every life change. Not only was she there to witness me grow as a person, but she is a big part of my growth even today. Of course, there are hardships with being a pet owner, so it is important to know what you are getting yourself into, but there are so many other unknown adventures that you will experience. Each pet has a unique personality, making owning pets so much fun.

"Dogs are better than human beings because they know but do not tell."

Emily Dickinson

BUDDY

SUMMER OF THE DOG

Sandy Pottorf

June was a month of unexpected changes that summer. My husband had resigned from his employment to pursue disability. My son suddenly needed a place to live and was staying with us. We had not expected his English Lab, Buddy.

That dog, all 125 pounds of him, would be residing in a house with three territorial cats. Buddy met this opposition as he entered our house for the first time. Highly pitched hissing greeted the intruder, who reacted by zipping ahead of the humans, scattering the felines in three different directions!

What could have been a humorous moment was instead an intense one. Caught off guard, Ray and I were speechless, and my son's raucous laughter did not help. Buddy was normally very obedient in our eyes, so we reasoned that if he stayed in the bedroom with his owner most of the time, it could work.

A dog in our house was definitely a new experience for me. I had never owned a dog although my husband had owned many and was probably looking forward to it. I was primarily concerned about how Buddy's presence would affect the cats.

Buddy's coloring was creamy with splotches of tan mostly on his back and head. When sitting it seemed that his constant tail-wagging would wind him up for take-off at every spoken word, and he always looked like he was sporting a wide grin.

The morning routine started out simple. Once my son left for work, Buddy waited patiently until there was movement in our room. Immediately he would plaster himself closely to the hallway door of his room. The felines gathered outside his door, at an untouchable distance from any doggie body fur or paws protruding under the door. One step of ours into the hallway was instant dismissal for them.

Buddy had never been tied up or leashed before; therefore, I had concern for his safety being loose outside, as we lived near a major highway. We requested a collar, leash and tether line be purchased, and used while he stayed with us.

If I was not working, Buddy was tethered right outside the kitchen door where we could see each other throughout the morning. The first few outings he barked and whimpered for attention, and usually got it. Gradually he became more interested in the newness of the smells around him.

Sometimes he and I would walk in laps around our spacious yard. Midway through the second or third cycle, the dog would usually seek out the shaded coolness under the towering white birch tree, where I would join him on my favorite bench.

One sultry evening when my son arrived home, he quickly changed clothes and went out to Buddy. The collar still attached to the tether cord had been removed and dropped on the ground, as the two boys ran off on some adventure.

Sometime later barking was heard in the front yard. There was my son, soaping up the back of that drenched and muddy dog!

Buddy had lunged into the neighbor's pond for a cold swim, followed by a doggie roll in some mud near the water. Now the cleaner pup and his human were lounging in the wet grass, aglow from the mischief. It might have been a Kodak moment if I had a camera, but at least I have the cherished memory.

Later that evening, when all the other humans and critters were snoozing, Buddy and I quietly sought out the birch tree, lazing by a lantern light. He crouched near my feet, his body resting against my leg. He needed me and I enjoyed feeling needed.

June soon became July, and still the son and dog were with us. Although alternating time with Buddy and his needs was enjoyable for us, we seemed to be turning into dog-sitters when my son wasn't around as expected.

One gorgeous summer day on my drive home from work, I got the notion that going to the lake would be a spontaneous escape for my husband and I. All I had to do was open the car door and Buddy had no hesitation in claiming his spot by stretching out the length of the seat.

My dubious husband wasn't sure he bought into my wacky plan. He was more interested in the indoor chill of air-conditioning than jumping into the hot car and driving off somewhere. He could see Buddy was ready for the car ride no matter what, and he reluctantly stated he couldn't "disappoint the dog".

When we got out of the car at the lake, it was obvious the objective of this trip was already met. While Ray and I were strolling along the water, enjoying the time and place after all, there was Buddy, sniffing, tasting, yanking the leash in an uncertain pattern as he investigated the beach. Laughter, sunlight, the beach, and that dog. A snippet of time recapturing earlier moments in our relationship.

Buddy had become our excuse to take more trips to the beach. Along with that dog, we met many folks, scattered along the breakwater built out into the little bay.

Ray would walk with Buddy along the paved walkway, while I putzed along taking snapshots of the scenery. Between the two of them they addressed almost every child, person, or dog along the way.

As we neared an older man sitting at the end of the break-way, Ray asked if he had caught anything yet. The guy hesitated a little bit before he grunted out one word—"Yeah". He seemed unimpressed that we dared to interrupt his pretty view of the setting sun spanning across the shimmering water. Buddy took the advantage of that one word, to slather his fat, sloppy tongue across the side of the man's face before plopping down next to him.

The man guffawed out a giggle before we could scold the dog. The two sat together like old buddies; the thumping tail on the pavement, the arm around the big dog that for a few heart-beats, sharing a fishing spot in the setting sun.

Not every whim of mine for the beach was instant hit with my husband. One such time, I expressed my idea to my son as he arrived after work. He went inside, came back in shorts, teasing the dog, "Wanna go?" The dog was instantly up, barking and jumping around, while my son said, "Buddy says we are gonna go!" The boy, his dog, and me!

There was a spot on one of the dog's legs, raw from constant licking, and another spot growing on the opposite leg. For the first time since living with us, Buddy went to the veterinarian. She ordered meds for his legs and did some tests. The severest leg wound was wrapped protectively to allay Buddy's suspect-ed anxiety.

That night I was concerned about the dog that has inspired so many of us in a brief time. I couldn't sleep; I found him lying on a cool hardwood floor, and positioned myself as closely as I comfortably could, reasoning that gentle strokes of affection would soothe his suffering.

Buddy had not improved by morning. It took two strong men to help us get him into the car one more time. It also took a gurney with two nurses to carry him into the vet's examination room.

The doctor explained Buddy would be staying at least one night. The diagnosis was diabetic ketoacidosis, or DKA, which was advanced. We were to call the next morning for an update.

My son went to visit his Buddy the next day. He called me, requesting me to make the arrangements so his dog would not be suffering anymore. He just felt he could not do it himself.

Because it was Friday the doctor would not be in the office much longer, I was already on my way, so she promised to wait,

Sitting on the floor beside him, I touched his face, ears, and snout; his eyes fluttered slightly.

"Are you ready to go home, Bud?" I asked. His paw lightly bumped my hand, just before I used it to wipe my tears.

That summer we shared with that dog will never be forgotten. That precious dog was a peacemaker in a household that, as a family, needed to be reminded how to love on each other again. How to forgive, be gracious, and move on. WE thought WE were providing that dog with a safe, loving environment during rough spots in his life; but I fervently believe our loving God gifted us the best lesson when He arranged for that dog to exemplify unconditional love to us instead.

"A dog is the only thing on earth that loves you more than you love yourself."

Josh Billings

SYDNEY

SYDNEY, THE WONDER DOG

Rita Preston

Sydney. Syd. The Wonder Dog. Daddy's Girl. Syd-Syd.

So many names for our sweet little girl. Based on her biological parents, she was designated as an Australian Shepherd, and our son's military family named her Sydney.

Sydney was a phenomenal girl. Our son warned us on Christmas Eve 2005 as he picked us up at the airport that her standing wiggle on the storm door would remind me of my late Sheltie mix, Frosty. She did!

Syd was beautiful, short-haired, born with a cropped tail and investigative nature. Her mostly black coat with white toes and white ascot lent an aristocratic air to her posture.

We took treat bones to help her get to know us. She would bury the bones in their giant sofa, and my hubby would move them. She raced through their house, looking in every crevice for her missing bones. Finding them on the sofa cushions, she glared at hubby and began new burying!

We met our newest granddaughter on that trip; she was four days old. Sydney was 8-10 months old. Syd was a mama figure full of youthful exuberance and worried about the new baby.

Sydney and her housemate Mel (who joined the family two months later) had adventures on the Pacific Ocean beach as often as the military schedule permitted. Syd and Mel traveled across the entire USA when duty stations changed. The dogs loved rocking out in the car, tunes up, noses out the windows, and cruising down the highway.

In Washington, DC, a second-floor apartment became home. When duty calls, military families adapt and overcome. The family found a good place to go for walks.

At some point, Syd developed seizures. She'd do her best to let her humans know just before a seizure hit, but she couldn't stop them. Finally, her loving human parents took her to the veterinarian, and she was prescribed a costly anti-seizure medication.

Sydney mothered, mentored, and bossed Melbourne; she was the Alpha. Mel, being younger, waited for her cues.

Fast forward a few years, Syd's seizures had increased. Her beloved family did not want her to suffer. We offered to bring her to 'the farm' and lay her to rest with our other critters. Our lady vet and 'Mel's girls' would treat her well.

Syd came for a week's vacation with our granddaughter and made it clear, her work on God's earth was not finished. During her visit, she was seizure-free. We visited the vet, updated her meds, and she continued to stay with us, monitoring her health.

Our vet indicated Syd had to be of Aussie Cattle Dog heritage. No matter her heritage, we all love her (love never dies).

She ran in the yard and played with Mel. They were still the best chums! Our son asked if this living arrangement could continue. Unanimously we said, "Sure"!

Mel taught Sydney about groundhogs and hunting. Then, one day, she tree'd her first groundhog. As I cleaned the stains from her fur, I assured her I was proud of her. Her nub of a tail wagged with joy.

They tag-teamed the 'evil critters' that dug holes in their playground. Mel was good for the sprint, and Syd, for the marathon. Mel would find the varmint, and initiate the pursuit, while Syd took the relay baton straight to any hole the critter found.

She could sit for hours, keeping watch. Then, if we approached her, she would snap her neck, glare, and return to duty. There was no greater guardian than Sydney.

Sydney was Daddy's girl; just as she had been more attached to our son in their home, she was also attached to Daddy here.

Syd and I had a talk when she moved in. I explained that she had been Alpha Dog in their other home, but Mel moved here first, so he was Alpha now. She consented without reminders, adapted, and overcame.

Herding dogs must be kept busy, or they find things. We had broken Mel of dumpster diving into our kitchen trash. After Syd's arrival, we suddenly found trash strewn across the kitchen. Hubby blamed Mel. Mel knew better, but his guilty look was unmatched. I insisted Sydney was instigating.

After much thought and work with the pups, the situation was resolved. We learned to be better humans and remove big temptations like chicken parts in the bin. Trash was carried outside, even if it wasn't full. Doggies and humans learned, adapted, and overcame.

Syd was older than Mel, but Mel had a defective heart. Syd had an occasional seizure, but it was rare. So, our vet surmised that she was burning off more energy with our big farmyard than when she was a city girl.

During an emergency trip, we left Syd and Mel with our kids in DC while we traveled. They were blessed to have a house with a yard again. Our son asked if they could keep Sydney. Knowing they missed her, answering was agony.

Our answer was a difficult one: No. Sydney and Melbourne would stay together, returning home to our rural home. Of course, they could always visit, but she had done well with our big yard. We are forever thankful that our son's family understood to keep Sydney and Mel together. Syd and Mel were best buddies.

When Mel succumbed to cancer, we left his little rosewood box of ashes on the coffee table for weeks so Syd could sniff. Mel's box found its home on our headboard, and Syd always had free access.

Sydney found a solo life without Mel. We played; we still rode in the car. She snuggled, mostly with Daddy. After all, she was Daddy's girl!

In 2018, I broke a hip. After a few weeks in hospital rehab, Daddy brought me home. When he needed to leave me, he would tell Sydney, "Keep an eye on Mummy!"

Syd would hop on a nearby chair and stare at me until he returned, no matter how long, 20 minutes or two hours, just like when she stood watch at a groundhog hole. Daddy would return and thank her. She would jump off the chair and flop on her bed at the foot of my hospital bed. We'd hear her huge sigh as she fell asleep, off-duty, and gentle ladylike snores ensued.

During my recovery, Sydney became Mama's Good Guard Girl. She was still Daddy's Girl, but we had evolved. I believe my recovery has aged her. She was a worrier, much like my human mom. Moms tend not to admit it, but they worry. Hubby says my injury didn't age her (to soften my heartache), but I believe she mothered me, her worrying aging her.

Sydney continued being our Wonder Dog for the next few years, but her age showed. Arthritis. Cataracts. We tried prescribed medications, trips to our chiropractor, and natural supplements to comfort her.

The pandemic hit. Syd was embarrassed not always being able to control natural functions. Her orthopedic bed was laundered frequently, and protective padding became normal. If we were going somewhere in the car, Syd was willing to go, even if she didn't stick her nose out of the window anymore. Just being with her people and listening to tunes was enough.

Her military family retired from active duty and moved nearby, so she saw them more often. She loved the snuggles from those who visited, especially our son. No longer could she see them clearly, but she knew they were hers, and she was theirs. She was loved and returned that love.

The pandemic continued, and in-person, in-puppy visits were not permitted at the veterinarian hospital. Instead, humans had to stay in vehicles while pets met with the doctor. It was insufferable. The vet knew. We knew. Syd knew.

Syd was nervous about the vet. Mel hadn't convinced her that 'his girls' were good and not to be afraid. So, she remained nervous, and that was that.

Our hearts ached. I insisted I would continue her hospice care forever if we couldn't be together at 'that moment.' I wouldn't let her go through the final moment alone. That was My decree. She understood, but she was fading.

Daddy made the call. We could be with her outside. Our son joined us. He took one final photo with her in the back seat, and Sydney smiled in that photo with her first Daddy. She hadn't 'smiled' in a long time. Always camera shy, Syd's smiles were golden, but she smiled for him. That is love.

Syd noshed on bacon that day. She knew it was the final delicious, perfect treat.

She was not alone. We three were there. Tears fell. One by one, her daddies stepped back and left me with my Good Guard Girl. Sydney's tee shirt said, "Mama's Good Guard Girl," It kept her calm during thunderstorms.

Sydney is The Wonder Dog she was destined to be. She plays with Mel again, catching frisbees and tennis balls, frolicking in heaven's snow.

"A dog is the only thing that can mend a crack in your broken heart."

Judy Desmond

MEL

MEL, THE SUPER DOG

Rita Preston

Mel was an Australian Shepherd; hence our son named him Melbourne. His military family adopted him on my birthday, a couple of months after we met their first Aussie, Sydney.

Melbourne came to live with us one fine winter's day.

He rode home in Daddy's semi-tractor.

His first daddy, a career Marine, patted the side of the truck and said, "Up." Mel climbed the steps like he'd climbed a ladder every day of his life.

Daddy called me (Mummy) and said he'd be home in about an hour and to meet him at the house. I left my office and waited. Mel and Daddy arrived, Mel's plumy tail, his pretty boy sashay across the yard and into his new abode. Daddy headed back to work, and I to my office. "WOOF. WOOF-WOOF. WOOF! WOOF-WOOF!!"

Our son assured us the barking would subside as Mel handled separation anxiety. Twenty minutes later and Mel was still woofing.

I returned to the house and discussed the worrying and woofing. He needed me to know he would not be left alone. So, we headed to my office with leash in hand, water bowl, and blankie.

My colleagues were joyous in welcoming Mel. They would inform me how he cried when I had to dash to the bank or post office without him; daily, "Mel jaunts" now covered the office errands. The 'girls' at the bank fussed about who would give Mel his daily treat!

I tried leaving Mel at home again. I returned one day, opened his crate so we could head outside, and realized there was no plumy tail waving in the winter wind. "Mel, where is your tail?" I bellowed! He ran to me with his pretty gait, wagged a very naked tail, and joined me inside. "Mel, where is your tail?" No fur. No hair. Nothing.

I called the veterinarian in panic mode. "Mel has no hair on his tail. He was in the crate all day. There is no hair anywhere!" The vet's office assured me that separation anxiety probably caused him to chew off all the hair from his tail but not to worry too much. It would pass, one way or another, from the front or the back end. It did.

Doggie hairballs are a whole new ballgame! But it did pass, more than once. We lived through it. Mel went back to work with me.

He loved car rides. Windows down, face and nose fully extended, snorting the air like a coke addict. I reminded him countless times that he would snort a bee, which wouldn't be a good thing. He never worried.

I pestered Daddy (my Hubby, an 'old' Marine) to get a sidecar for our Harley Ultra (Harley-DavidsonTM) to take Mel with us. Mel's ears would perk, and I knew Daddy was within 2-3 miles of the house. When the Harley pulled into the driveway, Mel was at the door, ready to greet Daddy.

One day, Daddy patted the seat, "Up!" Mel was on the seat like a lightning bolt and ready to ride! We smiled and laughed. I turned on the camera, and Mel posed. Yes, he posed. One paw up on a handlebar as if he owned the camera lens.

We realized that Mel's super-sensitive ears couldn't tolerate some of the pitches in the engine. He wanted to go with us; he would hop on the bike. He loved the wind on his face but not the sound. So, no sidecar. But, oh, the greetings and love when we returned home from a ride!

Once a year, we camped and rode in an annual ride in Washington, DC: Rolling ThunderTM. On those long Memorial Day weekends, Mel got to go "camping" too. He went to the local veterinarian's hospital with 'his girls.' He loved the ladies at the clinic.

I would ask him if he was ready to go camping, and his tail would start wagging.

Mel had a heart murmur. That was one reason Mel stayed at the vet when we traveled-his heart condition could be monitored. In addition, his heart condition explained a behavior we had found peculiar.

Mel loved to chase and retrieve tennis balls. After several throws, Mel would plop down, front paws crossed on top of the ball. After that, playing ball until he had caught his breath and jumped up, his terms.

The heart murmur diagnosis explained Mel's super smartness.

Hubby and I came home from a friend's house and chatted about how their dog, Digger, tackled groundhogs and other critters in their backyard. Less than a week later, Hubby came to our door, "Honey, come see this." Mel had conquered his first groundhog. Snapped its neck and came to show Daddy.

He didn't try to eat it, simply dispatched it from digging any more holes on our property. We laughed. All it had taken was for Mel to hear about a fellow canine tackling such beasts, and Mel was all in. Super dog!

One dark bitter winter's night after work, I rolled a tennis ball in the living room. Mel put a paw on it and nudged it with his nose in my direction. I rolled it back. He did it again. Tired from the office, I sat on the floor, legs stretched out, and rolled the ball back. Mel returned it. Mel was teaching me his own game!

Another day, Hubby called from his upstairs office, "I need my calculator!" I handed Mel the calculator, instructing, "Take it to Daddy!" Mel tried. Up the stairs, he went. Sadly, he dropped the calculator on the landing and, in desperation, chomped on it. He took it into Daddy's office with a no longer functional display.

We decided to try something else. I turned a can of soda pop sideways and handed it to Mel, who took the cold beverage in his firm jaws. Then, he headed to the living room. The can was cold. It slipped. His jaws tightened to avoid dropping the can, puncturing the aluminum and root beer sprayed everywhere!!

I ran for towels. Hubby laughed and announced, "No hurry, Mel likes root beer!" Sure enough, Mel was lapping up the sweet sticky carbonation. We practiced: empty cans, cold empty cans, filled cans, and eventually cold filled cans.

The next time our son visited, I asked Mel if he'd like to 'get daddy a beer?' Mel trotted to the kitchen and returned, proudly carrying a soda in his mouth. Our son was mortified, "You taught my dog to carry a beer?"

We laughed! "It's only root beer, and he's our dog now."

Our kids loved Mel, but Mel was a big boy and strong. They had a toddler. Mel had learned to jump baby gates, and the toddler ended up with a bloodied nose. Mel had no clue how strong he was, and toddlers have no clue about big doggies.

They wanted Mel to be loved. They were glad we offered to take Mel to the country where he could run. When Mel had joined their little clan, they'd had a house with a yard. One military transfer later, they were in a 2nd-floor apartment, a tough den for a herding dog.

Mel went swimming with the geese at our brother's pond. We forgot they told us he liked to swim in the ocean! He rode home in the truck bed covered in things from the pond. Mel liked smelly things. He found a dead skunk in a road ditch. Hubby spotted him on his back, all four feet in the air, happily wiggling to and fro. (I found them in the backyard after the bath, with Hubs muttering, "You are a dumb, dumb dog," and other affectionate things!

We thought we understood why our son's family had nicknamed him "Smelly Melly."

Mel still loved car rides and snorting air like an air addict. Truly, he smelled everything. He was a smelly dog!

Mel had a tiny tumor on his chest. One summer, it enlarged. A biopsy was done and revealed cancer.

Holistic supplements. Love. Playtime when he had the energy. Our chiropractor gave Mel adjustments—anything to provide quality of life.

Winter came, and the cancer returned. Again, we conferred with his doctor and did all we could to provide comfort and love. He wore protective tee-shirts (tie-dyed to the military) with pride.

Cancer was exhausting all of us and, worse yet, was winning the war.

When we arrived at the hospital, Mel's girls waited lovingly for their boy. A few minutes later, we were with him on a blanket, and we told him we loved him forever.

Mum gently placed her Best Boy's head on his paw and sobbed a flood of tears into that beautiful merle coat.

Mel romps with Sydney and doesn't get winded chasing tennis balls and frisbees. I know he forgave me for not curing him. He is forever my Best Boy.

*"Time spent with cats
is never wasted."*

Sigmund Freud

KITSIE

IT'S A KITSIE KIND OF DAY

Coree Sullivan

I love the quiet in the house early in the morning before the sun comes up. The phone is quiet, my Human isn't hustling around the house getting ready for a meeting, the neighbors are catching the last of their sleep before guarding their homes, it's just peaceful and quiet.

What a great time to plan my day! I have a lot of 'to do's' on my list, you know. After all, I am the Cat in Charge around here!

First, I need my Human to get up and feed me. That's sometimes a challenge. You'd think she only sleeps to prolong my hunger pains in the morning!

She's a nice Human, don't get me wrong. She always makes sure there's plenty of my favorite foods around for me to eat. She let's me outside for a while everyday so I can have my hunting time, which is the best part of my day, in my book.

She doesn't yell at me and is always there to give me a pat on the head or a snuggle when I allow it or course. Plus, if I wander a bit too far from our house, she always comes to find me, so I don't have to ever worry about getting too lost. She seems

90

to know my favorite outdoor hiding places to take a nice after-noon nap.

The next thing I need to do today is to be sure to get outside early so I can catch the morning sun in one of my favorite nap-ping areas. That spot is so peaceful! It's under a Blue Spruce tree just outside our yard in the greenbelt. The sun is so warm, and I'm well camouflaged with the lower hanging branches. I feel safe there as I take a short nap.

One thing I like to do is watch for bugs to chase. It's always great entertainment when I capture one and it plays a game of hide and seek with me between the blades of grass. Sometimes I find bugs that fly. Those are my favorite because I get to run more and jump high into the air to catch them, or at least bat them down to the ground.

I don't want to hurt them, so I let them go after a while. I just want to share part of my day with them as we play. I'm always very careful to recognize what kind of a bug they are by the way. You know I wouldn't want to play with a bee or a wasp. They don't play fair with their little stingers. I learned that the hard way!

Around noon everyday my Human comes out to talk with the neighbor over the fence. She has two dogs that like to bark at me. I don't get too close to them. You never know when that fence is going to give way and those dogs will chase me. Maybe even bite me! Nope...I give all dogs, big or small, a wide berth when I see them. I might even give them a warning hiss just to let them know I'm just not any old cat and if they're smart, they won't tangle with me.

Sometimes I'm out in the backyard when the neighbor's dogs are out. My favorite thing to do with them is to sit in the mid-dle of my backyard and just stretch or lay there watching them.

They get so worked up with all their barking and carrying on! It's so much fun!

In the afternoon, after so much activity, I need a nap. So, I find a quiet, safe place in the house like a closet or under the bed to just relax and fall asleep for a couple of hours.

Sometimes in my time of sleep I have crazy dreams. I'm chasing huge bugs through tall grass and my legs and/or whiskers start to twitch. Sometimes I even let out a muffled growl or hiss because the dream is so real! I don't remember much about it after I wake up. It was just a 'sleep adventure'.

After my nap my Human is good about giving me a snack. She gives me these really yummy, moist snacks that taste like chicken, which is my favorite food.

I'm a pretty picky eater. I don't like turkey or fish, but I love various forms of chicken and beef foods. My Human always has a good assortment and I appreciate her for that. It lets me know she hears me, and I am in charge because she wants to please me.

After my snack, I like to go out and play in the backyard again for a while. I always hope I see a butterfly. Those are my favorite! They look so graceful as they flit from flower to flower. I'm fascinated by them! I try to play with them. I stalk them. Then I run and jump to try to bat at them, but they always elude me. Then I chase them through the yard jumping now and then to try and reach them. After a while I just lay down and watch them in all their splendor.

If the neighbor dogs are out, I tease them for entertainment. Sometimes I just lay on the patio and watch the world go by thinking how awesome it is that I am the Cat in Charge. The world is my oyster, and all of this is for my entertainment and enjoyment. It's good to be me!

Around the end of the day, I go back in and see what my Human is up to. Sometimes she's busy so I just go check for any morsels of food left over from earlier, then go take a short nap. I know soon she will be making her dinner and bring me some more amazing cat food to eat while she eats her Human food.

After dinner she sometimes takes a walk, so I'm stuck in the house until she gets back. But there are a lot of things I need to check on to be sure all is well and in place. There's always the basement that needs investigating. I usually spend my time on the main floor, but the basement needs attention too, so I make sure to go down there, sniff at the storage boxes. Sometimes jump on top of them and lay down to survey everything from my perch which is really my throne.

Then I hear my Human coming in the garage and dash upstairs to greet her at the door. I don't ever want her to think I don't appreciate her coming home to take care of me and meet my needs!

Then we settled down in the living room for our evening to-gether. She is on her laptop often, so I find a place close to her to make sure she's ok. Sometimes she decides to watch a mov-ie on TV, so I sit in the overstuffed chair next to the couch, where she's sitting, and we have an evening together.

Then it's time for bed. My Human checks my food bowl to be sure I have something to snack on in the night when I'm up to do my patrol around the house. I check to be sure she's sleep-ing well, and nothing is disturbing her. I check on the doors by sniffing them to be sure nothing is on the other side that would bring her harm while she's resting.

Then I lay down for my evening sleep. I need it after such a busy day! As I drift off to sleep, I think to myself, 'it's good to be the Cat in Charge'!

"A dog is the only thing on earth that loves you more than you love yourself."

Josh Billings

DUKE

COOLING DOWN DUKE

Coree Sullivan

It was a hot, dry day. The sun was relentless with its bright rays. There was no escape for Duke, a 120 lb. St. Bernard. It seemed he couldn't pant fast enough or hard enough to get cooled down.

Duke wandered from the back porch on the north side of the house, which provided ample shade, to inside the barn to lay on the straw, which temporarily provided some relief. Then out to the lawn to lie under the shade tree and hope for a little breeze.

He was such a grand St. Bernard. His eyes were kind and loving until they saw a rabbit that needed chasing. Then his eyes were pinpoint focused on chasing it down, only to end up frustrated as it disappeared down its rabbit hole.

His morning routine consisted of food first, of course. After all, it takes a good amount of food to give this big boy the energy he needs to complete his day! After breakfast, Duke would check on the chickens first in case they needed some chasing to keep them in line.

His next stop was to see what, if anything, had changed in the barn. Was Bully, the pony, inside or out in the corral? Bully got her name honestly; she was a Quarter-Shetland horse mix and could be stubborn and onery when she wanted to be.

Bully allowed our girls to ride her for a walk, but she wasn't up for a trot very often. She was getting on in age, and trotting or even a gallop was not on her menu of activities. But she seemed to like Duke and his company when he visited her. Maybe his size made her think he was a pony too!

Duke would saunter around the corral, smelling little things like straw, weeds, and Bully droppings. Then snort and walk away. Bully often followed Duke around to ensure she wasn't missing out on delicacies. After all, Bully was a horse. A small one, but she came with a horse's appetite!

After visiting Bully, Duke would walk the perimeter of the 2-acre parcel we lived on. He did this pretty much every day, no matter what the weather was like. However, if it was in the winter and we were having a blizzard, we wouldn't allow him out for any longer than to do his business and come back in.

On this 98-degree day, poor Duke had just had it. After all, it had been in the high 90s for almost three weeks, with little breezes occasionally but not enough to cool him down. So, Duke decided, while no one was watching, to explore a place to hang out that would help him get some relief.

I had been in the house focusing on cleaning, laundry, and ensuring my daughters were playing together well. Then, if all went well, I would turn on the full-blast sprinkler in the front yard for the girls and Duke to run through. But that wouldn't be until after nap time, so Duke was left to his own devices. The truth is, I had forgotten entirely about checking on what Duke was up to.

After about an hour, it crossed my mind that Duke hadn't returned to lay on the porch in the shade. I had taken out a big bowl of water with ice for him, but he was nowhere to be found. I called, but he didn't come. I didn't get too worried about it. "He probably found a cool place to rest and is taking a nap," I thought and returned to my house chores.

Not more than 10 minutes later, the phone rang. I went to answer it, and my neighbor, from across the road, was on the other line and was not happy! It seemed as though Duke found the perfect place to cool down. In my neighbor's irrigation ditch that was running full blast to irrigate his corn!

I checked on the girls and told them I was going out front, across the road, and they were to stay in the house. But of course, they followed me to see what all the excitement was about.

There, across the road from the driveway, was Duke, lying in the irrigation ditch and expensive irrigation water flowing up over the banks on either side of him. He looked so happy to be cool, finally!

My neighbor was not quite so happy. The water had spilled into the barrow pit on one side and was wasted. The water on the other side had begun to wash out the little ditches that guided the water down through the rows of corn.

Immediately I scolded Duke for causing such a mess with my outside voice. But my inside voice was giggling at the site he had created. However, Duke knew by the tone of my voice that he was in trouble and jumped up and out of the ditch. He then covered both my neighbor and me with water that remained on his coat.

My daughters had stayed obediently across the road but had a full view of everything happening. They had laughed so hard they were sitting on the ground now, still laughing at Duke and the situation he had caused.

I asked my neighbor if he had an extra shovel and immediately started building up the banks of the big ditch so the water would stay in it. Then I helped him shore up the little ditches between the rows of corn so the water would stay in them. After that, I helped him set the tubes and get them running again.

Whew! Being in the cool water felt good, but cleaning up Duke's mess was a lot of work! My neighbor and I laughed about it a few weeks later. Poor Duke, he just wanted to cool off.

The next day I bought two kiddie pools; one for my girls to play in and one for Duke to cool off in. He sure looked much happier on the hot days that followed, being able to lay in his pool and cool off. Of course, Duke had to be kept on a leash after discovering the ditch across the road so the crops could get watered properly and no more breaking ditch banks down.

We set up Duke's pool well within reach of his leash, under the shade tree he loved. It's been a few decades since that day, but we still talk fondly of Duke's adventures that hot summer day.

A couple of years later, we sold that home and the acreage to a sweet young couple with a German Shepard. Before the closing, we decided to see how the dogs got along because taking Duke with us on the move was impossible.

The German Shepard was named Sargent. He was very sweet-tempered and full of energy. When he and Duke met, it was as if they had been buddies for years! So, we left Duke with the buyers and Sargent. We told them about Duke's creativity in cooling down in the irrigation ditch across the road and that we needed to keep him on a leash but within reach of a baby pool full of cool water so he could cool down when he wanted.

A few years later, when Duke was 12, I received a letter from the buyers saying Duke had crossed the rainbow bridge. Duke would be missed, but the current owners had their own adventures with Duke that they could share. Duke was quite the dog!

Dogs are not our whole life, but they make our lives whole.

Roger Caras

COCOA

LOVE, HEARTBREAK, HEALING

Amy Walston

I never intended to get a dog; it was not on my agenda. Instead, I had a small fish tank with a beautiful blue fish swimming lazily around. Watching him float with the air bubbles moving to the surface was calming. I kept a snail with him to help keep the tank clean.

For some reason, the snails did not live long. I remember it was a Sunday in December, two weeks before Christmas, and another snail had died. I went to the pet store to get a new one. In the center of the store, they had a little ring set up with puppies in the middle. Well, who can resist picking up a tiny little puppy? Not me, that's for sure. It was my undoing! I picked the smallest, most pathetic looking one in the bunch. She was so tiny. I held her close, and she fell asleep in my arms.

As my heart melted, a little girl ran up and cried, "There she is!". I replied, "Oh, did you want to hold her?" A very enthusiastic nod was the answer. I quickly gave her to the child, thinking she had saved me from falling for that little pup. I proceeded to pick out a snail and headed home.

Funny thing, I couldn't get that pup off my mind all day. I called the store near closing time and asked if she was still available. She was! I told them I was on my way. I left the store with the puppy, food, a crate, bowls, and everything I needed for the pup. I'm sure I made the owner's day with that sale! I drove home with her on my lap and asked her what I should call her. I started saying names. When I said Cocoa, she looked up at me. Ok, then, Cocoa it is! That was the start of my love affair with the best little doggie in the whole wide world. My Cocoa girl.

Cocoa was a sheltie-miniature poodle mix. She looked like the smallest collie you have ever seen. She was so pretty. I trained her to go in a litter box. That way, we never had to go outside in crappy weather when she had to go. On days I had to work late, I never worried about her as all her needs were taken care of. She had food, water, a bed, and the litter box in her space. The only other thing she needed was me.

I binge-watched episodes of the Dog Whisperer to learn how to train her. Teaching her to walk on a leash gave her much freedom and fun. She was my walking buddy. We went on power walks together almost daily when the weather was nice. She had the stamina to go with me for an hour at a time. I loved it. I probably would not have gone for those long walks by myself. For some reason, I would have felt self-conscious walking alone. With her by my side, I had the freedom to enjoy long walks in different neighborhoods, and our favorite place to walk was the old cemetery. That cemetery was huge with hills and curves.

Cocoa was my traveling companion. We once traveled from Ohio to Surfside, South Carolina. She did great on the drive there. She didn't complain, but she would look at me and sigh as if to say, "Seriously, are we there yet? This is getting old."

She loved the beach. We took long walks along the shore-line where the water was lapping up. She had a blast. It was so much fun for me to watch her prance through the water. It made vacationing alone fun.

The house I rented had a pool, another first for Cocoa. At first, she didn't know what to think about being in the water. I would hold her and let her float around. She finally relaxed and en-joyed it and began to smile. I got such a kick out of her—my little buddy.

It always amazed me how observant Cocoa was. She watched me do everything. She studied my facial expressions. If I were upset or mad about something, she would slink out of the room without me saying a word. She saw my face. I would have to go get her and hug her to let her know I wasn't upset with her. She watched what clothes I put on. I don't understand how she knew my work clothes from my relaxation clothes. But she did. When I got home from work, I would change out of my work clothes and put on my soft comfy clothes if I was in for the evening. If I was going out, I put on an outfit. She would watch me change out of my clothes and watch me put on something else. She would get upset if I put an outfit on and not my com-fies! She knew I was leaving her without me saying a word. It blew my mind her powers of observation. She knew me.

She was my confidant! I talked to her non-stop. All day long, I told her everything. She was one smart dog with a huge vocab-ulary. Yet, our connection was one I had never experienced with another human being, let alone a canine. Cocoa was the child I never had. She was my little girl. My baby. She was everything to me.

When she was 14, she started having issues with her kidneys. Protein was restricted, and her food was closely monitored to prolong her life. I bought more time with her by putting her on a restricted diet. She did improve for a few months. The vet said she should live another two years. She didn't last that long. It was heartbreaking to see her decline. She spent most of the day sleeping. On January 1st, 2020, I spent the day lying in bed with Cocoa and holding her. She flopped her head against my chest as if to say, "Oh, Mom, I'm done." I took her to the vet the next day. She agreed it was her time to go. I held her as they injected her to ease her passing. Tears flowed down my face as I felt her go. Her breathing became labored until it simply stopped. My daughter was gone. The best little doggie in the whole wide world left me and this earthly life.

It has been three years, and my heart is finally ready to let another little doggie in. I wish they lived as long as we do. That would be an unbelievable gift to have our fur babies with us for our lifetimes. I still miss her. I am trying to move on.

As of this writing, I brought a new puppy home two weeks ago. Her name is Calle, and she is an ornery little girl! Cocoa can never be replaced, but with Calle, a new saga is beginning.

"Pets are not our whole lives, but they make our lives whole."

Roger Caras

PUMPKIN

A CHANGE OF HEART

by Amy Zdilla

"Oh, you'll understand one day."

I must tell you; I just didn't understand. As I was strolling around the neighborhood and conversing with my husband, I could only reply: "I don't get it."

I couldn't relate to his stories from his childhood of having this special bond with his sweet and sly boxer, Molly. He told me funny stories about her and, sadly, how heartbreaking it was when she was no longer around.

On the contrary, my childhood years were different than his. The occasional goldfish would make its way into our home, but that is where it stopped. I didn't develop a bond with my fish as he did with his dog.

"Yeah, I don't see it. Whatever." I replied.

Let's fast forward several years in marriage and life when I began to have a change of heart and feel a bond I didn't know existed.

When making large decisions, my husband and I are not very spontaneous. However, in this instance, we were! The universe pushed us to make one of the best spontaneous decisions ever, and things began to change for me.

We were made aware that "Pumpkin" was available and ready for a home. How could two people who met on Halloween say no to a tiny puppy named "Pumpkin!" We took that as a sign that we were all meant to be together, and the decision was made.

As I've grown in age and life experiences, I've realized that with every life stage, we learn a lesson. Although sometimes hard to realize, the universe presents us with things when the time is right, and everything happens for a reason. I believe this is what happened here.

With that said, two days later, we traveled from morning to night to pick up this 5-pound Mini Goldendoodle named Pumpkin.

Our hearts were full of love from day one with her quiet puppy whimpers and silly personality. So why was this not part of my life for the first 38 years?

We can't change the past, but we can change how the present and future look and feel. We must find things along our journey that enrich our lives and bring us joy. After 38 years, it was time to add this wonderful new joy to my life.

It's not always easy finding joy in life's ups and downs, but it is imperative that we do so.

Joy isn't the absence of disease or the absence of sickness; it's about finding pockets of time and experiences that bring us genuine happiness. It's also about finding things that make us pause, enjoy the moment, and give us an internal spark.

To feel completely happy, satisfied, and fulfilled as humans, we must explore ways to do this beyond just the basic everyday necessities and things within our comfort zone. We must seek out ways to find this joyful spark inside and keep it going.

We must engage in activities that fulfill us regularly and enrich our days. In essence, find our true joys.

Few things in life bring us as much joy and contentment as having a dog. Dogs truly go above and beyond for us; it is difficult to relate until we experience their presence.

Pumpkin's silly attitude like, "side eyes," how she says "I want more food" by trotting around with an empty bowl in her mouth, and how she "barters" for treats by dropping toys at your feet, fill my soul with joy.

It all makes sense, and I can now relate to the love our canine companions bring to our lives. Pumpkin has enriched my life in many more ways than one:

1. She makes me smile every morning. Regardless of how I slept, what's on my mind, or whatever thoughts I have about the day ahead, I start my day with a smile and an instant dose of Vitamin Pumpkin.

2. She provides free therapy. We all suffer from stress at some point. For me, there was a time when the world was heavy. Pumpkin provided the pure love and therapy my mind and body needed. She listened non-judgmentally, provided unconditional love, boosted oxytocin (the feel-good hormone) and gave me immediate injections of joy. It was apparent that having this little fur baby increased positivity and decreased negativity in my life and this was a huge win—win in my eyes!

3. She brings out my playful side. A little chase around the dining room table, a good game of fetch and "toy tug" bring out my inner child and a refreshing playfulness we typically don't experience.

4. She encourages happy energy and positive vibes. Her silliness, playfulness, and big round puppy eyes make our home feel alive and vibrant. Our home environment can fuel or drain us, and having a pup provides a positive home energy like none other. Once your eyes have been awakened to this energy, a home without a pup seems rather foreign. As they say, "In a perfect world, every home would have a dog, and every dog would have a home."

5. She fills a void. The universe said no to little feet running around our home, but it did say yes to little paws running around our home, and for that, I'm grateful. She gave me the perfect chance to nurture and feel needed. Our dogs rely on us for everything, and when they're supported and happy, we're supported, happy, and fulfilled.

6. She cleans my plate. I can always count on her to clean my breakfast or dinner plate. Eggs, Brussels sprouts, or pizza crust have no chance if left uneaten on my plate. But who really can say no to puppy eyes asking for a morsel of leftover food?!

7. She is a physical fitness companion. Everyone needs to stay active, and a dog is a built-in motivator. She makes me want to be healthier. It's hard not to stay active when your dog is begging to get outside. On days when I'm not feeling motivated, her excitement and wagging tail encourage me to go for a neighborhood walk.

8. She makes me laugh (All.The.Time.). Dogs are funny creatures! I may be partial, but Pumpkin is hysterical. In my father's words, "She is a laugh a minute," I fully agree! I can't contain a smile when her head tilts, saying, "Tell me more" and her sleeping positions say, "I'm letting it all hang out."

9. She has become one of the family. Isn't it true we are adamant that our dogs won't ever be allowed on that couch, in that room, or in that car? So inevitably, they end up on that couch, in that room, and in that car, which happened in our home. She fits right in and is now "one of the family."

10. She provides for a better life. Finally, this is the simplest and most self-explanatory reason, she makes life better.

We often don't realize what we're missing until we find it. For me, it was about taking a chance to realize something that I once didn't understand. It was about finding the purest joy and enjoying it wholeheartedly.

I'm a different person because of Pumpkin, and I will be forever grateful for that.

Maybe you are like I was years ago—not understanding, not feeling this bond, or getting it.

Remember, your fur angel could be out there waiting to fill your heart and feed your soul. Allow yourself to witness and experience the meaning of "man's best friend"!

I know I have.

GOODBYE IS THE HARDEST PART

by Kim Lengling

Oh goodness. We have all been there, saying a final goodbye to our fur babies.

I have found over the years that it does not get any easier. But, gosh, it seems as if it gets more difficult!

But...having the opportunity to say goodbye. To be right there with our beloved pets as they head toward the Rainbow Bridge is an honor.

Our pets provided love, fun, laughter, joy, and on that final day, tears while they were a part of our lives.

But think of how different your life would have been had they not been a part of your life!

Please don't dwell on that final day, as sad as it is, and believe me, I have been there and done that!

I feel dwelling on that final day is a disservice to a beautiful soul who enriched and enhanced your life for years!

Their time with us is short, but they pack a lot of unconditional love into those years!

A SPECIAL VISIT

by Kim Lengling

It is a beautiful, wooded path with sunbeams shooting through the branches.

Mum walks along on her own, leaves crunching underfoot. She is overwhelmed by the beauty surrounding her and wonders how she got here.

Up ahead, she sees a flash of brilliant light and a dark shape rushing toward her.

Dig: Mum!! Mum!!

Mum: *Falling to her knees* Digger! Oh, my goodness, look at you, bud! You're young again and you are fast as lighting!

Dig: *Barking and Jumping, running in circles, licking Mum's face, filled with puppy-like joy* Mum! You are not going to believe what it's like here!

Mum: Where are we, Dig? It's beautiful!

Dig: Well, this is a special visit, so it's a special place. But I can't stay long.

Mum: But Dig...

Dig: *Overflowing with excitement, running back and forth in front of Mum,* "Mum! Guess who I am taking walks with? Guess! Guess!"

Mum: *Smiling and laughing* I don't know, bud. Who?

Dig: Who did you always talk to when we took our walks?

Mum: I prayed, Dig. I was talking to God.

Dig: Well, Mum, I'm taking walks with God! And you should see it there!

Mum: Oh, my goodness, Dig. Oh. My. Goodness.

Dig: *Jumping* Guess what else?

Mum: What else, sweet guy?

Dig: Well, while me and God were walking, I told him that you were probably sad without me. And you know what? He already knew!

Mum: *Listening to her Diggster share his story, unable to form any words*

Dig: *Jumps and snorts* And, I told him you were pretty stubborn.

Mum: Dig! You told God I was stubborn?!

Dig: *Snorts* Mum, He knew that too!

Mum: *Putting her head in her hands* Oh my gosh, Digger.

Dig: He laughed, Mum.

Mum: *Mouth dropping open* God laughed at me?

Dig: No, Mum, He laughed because of you. He knows you—everything about you.

Mum: Oh, Dig, I feel so happy and sad at the same time.

Dig: *Licking Mum on her face* Mum, do you know what happens when God laughs?

Mum: No, buddy, I don't.

Dig: All the souls sing, Mum. God laughs, and all the souls sing, and it's like all the love in all the world.

Mum: *Tears streaming down her face* Oh my goodness, Dig.

Dig: *Looking over his shoulder* Mum, I gotta go now, they're calling me.

Mum: But Dig.

Dig: *Jumping and running back and forth in excitement* Gotta go Mum! I'm going for another walk!

And off he runs, back down the path with the speed of a puppy. Suddenly, he leaps and turns in mid-air, facing his Mum.

Mum: *Sitting in the path while tears stream down her face*

Dig: Mum! Don't forget! All the love in all the world, and YOURS is here too! Love ya, Mum!

With a joyous bark, off he runs, turning back down the wooded path, running at top speed, and in a flash of brilliant white light, he disappears.

Mum awakes with a start, tears streaming down her face. She recalls the words: "All the souls sing, and it's like all the love in all the world, and YOURs is here too."

Smiling through her tears, she thanks God for "special visits" and the reminder that her Digger is well cared for, most definitely well-loved, and on the best adventure of his life.

CONCLUSION

Whew! What an emotional roller coaster, huh? But didn't you find yourself smiling or chuckling along the way?

Did one or more of the stories bring to mind a pet you had in your life? Maybe it was your first dog as a child or the first time your cat snuggled up against you.

Maybe it brought to mind those sweet moments of watching your pet sleep or do a big yawn and stretching when they first wake up.

Perhaps it brought to mind witnessing your dog's excitement for the beginning of a new day. Ready to take on whatever adventure you may experience together?

Although our animals' lives seem short, they are here for as long as they are meant to be. When we feel we had to say good-bye too soon, remember the love, so much love, packed into the years our beloved pets were with us.

I hope you enjoyed the stories in this book as much as I did when I read them!

THINGS TO CONSIDER
BEFORE YOU GET A PET

When choosing your family's pet, you should know what type of pet you want.

Several factors should go into making that decision.

* How old are your kids?
* How many people are in the house?
* How much time do you have?
* How much space do you have?
* How much energy do you have?
* Do you have the financial resources to care for a pet?

Owning a pet is a privilege that brings us great rewards. However, because our pets can't speak for themselves, we must each take on the responsibility as owners to advocate for them and provide the support and resources they need to live healthy, happy lives.

Providing that support begins even before we bring a pet home.

Source—AVMA (American Veterinary Medical Association)

Thank you for reading this book!

Did you enjoy this book? **Please leave a review***. Reviews are so helpful for authors!*

Other ways to help get the word out:

- *Share a link to the book or mention it on social media*
- *Pick up another copy to share with someone*
- *Recommend this book*

Visit www.kimlenglingauthor.com, and share your thoughts via the contact page. You can also find out what anthologies may open up next for a potential co-author, just like you!

AUTHOR PAGE

"Let's toss nuggets of hope into the world like confetti."

Email:
contact@kimlengingauthor.com

Website:
www.kimlengingauthor.com

Amazon Author Page:
https://www.amazon.com/Kim-Lengling/e/B00L9N6VBO

Let Fear Bounce Podcast:
https://anchor.fm/kim-lengling1

Let Fear Bounce FB Page:
https://www.facebook.com/letfearbouncepodcast

The Write Stuff TV Show FB Page:
https://www.facebook.com/TheWriteStuffTVShow

Do you have a story to share? Have you ever thought that you may want to be a published author?

Email contact@kimlenglingauthor.comto find out upcoming themes and get on the list for upcoming anthologies.

ABOUT THE AUTHOR

Sharing her faith, nature, and love of animals, and as a veteran living with PTSD, Kim is passionate about spreading and sharing nuggets of Hope through all of her endeavors.

Kim uses her experience of 25+ years in the corporate world as a part of the foundation for building her dreamw of writing, podcasting, and hosting a television show, sharing her story and others. Building platforms that help others to share their story and to spread Hope. The About Face Radio show, Let Fear Bounce, Tossing Nuggets of Hope, is the newest to her platforms.

Featured as a co-author in ten anthologies, Kim is the lead author and coordinator of a collaborative 3-book faith-based series titled When Grace Found Me. In addition, she has authored and coordinated a stand-alone, When Hope Found Me, and Paw Prints on the Couch anthology, releasing Summer of 2023.

She hosts the podcast Let Fear Bounce and a radio show with the same name. In addition, she hosts the TV Show, The Write Stuff, The Author's Voice with the Believe In Your Dreams

TV Network. She is also a co-host of a weekly radio show, Voices4Vets, in her local area.

You can regularly find Kim walking with her rescue dog, Dexter, reading, drinking coffee, and jotting down story ideas about her Realm. In addition to writing and being the Queen of her Realm, she is a 25+ year advocate for veterans providing support through monthly care packages for over 22 years.

Made in the USA
Columbia, SC
20 August 2023

21874711R00081